Maybe the Land Sings Back

Maybe the Land Sings Back
by Jan LaPerle
Copyright © Jan LaPerle 2022

ISBN 978-09817510-3-1

Songs
O for a Thousand Tongues to Sing (by Carl Glaser, arranged by John Carter)
Reveille
Orbits (by Wayne Shorter)

Cover Painting by Michael Carson, "Sticks and a Blue Dress"
Book design by Adam Robinson

Galileo Books
freegalileo.com

Maybe the Land Sings Back

Poems by Jan LaPerle

Galileo Press
Aiken, South Carolina

Table of Contents

Part Three

for Winnie

O for a Thousand Tongues to Sing

Spirited, but not too fast

In All Their Performances

My daughter
wakes.

Where are you,
she hollers.

I am everywhere,
I holler back

from some
backroom other

life I'd chosen
once,

some other street,
another house

moved to the next.
But how

would I be able to get
to you?

she asks.
Just like that,

I am here.

Everyone Thought We Were the Same Person

> I watch, and am as a sparrow alone upon the house top.
> *— Psalm 102*

My husband's home nurse, Stephanie,
has the smallest hands, like rain, almost,
like birds with their tiny bones flying in and out
so quietly from the feeder. They disappear.
Stephanie unhooks my husband from his chemo.
I'm waiting in the background. I sit on a bench;
I sit on a chair and crochet. My balls of yarn:
I've been talking to them quietly, but they keep
disappearing. I stitch a blanket, then hide under it.
I just turned 43. You wouldn't know it. I mean,
you would, but I just want to play and I can't.
I must sit and I've been feeling so small, a little girl
in a movie told her father after running away.
She didn't really want to go; she just wanted him
to come after her. In the window behind the girl,
the snow was falling. When I was young, the snow
was always falling. In the window behind Stephanie,
yellow leaves of the maple fall in the wind, fast as rain.
I'm shaken and small inside my day with my hands
pressed against the edges. My hands are small, too,
not as small as Stephanie's but just as warm, and the marks
I make from pressing so hard, they quickly disappear,
like my breath on the window where I wait,
from the edges, quietly.

Honeysuckle

Sometimes it's the ghost of my husband
after he's left me in the house alone,
his boots on the top shelf in his closet
looking caught when I open the door.
I always remember to button the top button
of his clean shirts when I hang them
so they don't fall in a wrinkly heap to the floor.
This morning from bed, the click of his hand flipping on
the nightlight in the dark bathroom made me feel
more loved than anything he's been trying these days,
and he's been trying. Like giving me the house
to myself this morning, just me and the old balloons
left over from our daughter's birthday party.
They drift silently across the floor. They hover
above the air vents and gather under the table
and chairs. This morning he said it is time
for the balloons to go. Hours later, after
all this time alone with them, I said I wasn't ready.
Earlier this year, after working out the details
of divorce, I said the same thing about leaving
and remember now how endings really are
that sudden. During one of our fights, I watched
our daughter from across the yard, edging
slowly along the honeysuckle bushes, picking flowers,
eating the honey, drops so small you can hardly
taste them. I remember her look as she glanced
back at us. That night, a heavy summer storm,
and in the morning I found the wildflowers
asleep on the grass. I cut them awake,
placed a jar of them next to the kitchen sink.
It was all I could do right then to look at them.

Cupboard

One day I decide I'll do something
good for people,
but I forget, then I nap.
My daughter wants to make
lemon cake so we do that.
I stand on the stool
and begin this great hunt
for poppy seeds.
Hours pass, and I'm on my tiptoes.
I stop searching for a minute to listen
to the wind. The branches snapping.
My daughter ran off again to her swing,
her swing tied to the branch
of the tree she climbs,
the tree run through with electric wires
in the yard she flies her kite in.
She flies it high as the cell tower.
Her dragon kite breathing fire.
Her dragon kite headed in a nosedive
straight into those electric lines.
I can't do anything about anything.
I'm trapped in the cupboard
forgetting what I'm searching for.
I dust the spice tops; they go on forever.
My hair too tight in its bobby pins.
Here as good as any place to pray.

Why I Dreamed My Dog Chased Me
Over the Ledge and Broke His Paw

Maybe it was pain, a root canal
the day before, fear worming all
through me, apples on the countertop
softening, or the sound of my baby
calling in the dark: *Mama! Mama?*
I ran to her, the door to the yard
wide open where she stood
pointing in the dark. *I wish so bad*
someone would shoot the moon, slow all this down.
I sent her to school, two bags of candy
in her backpack. I didn't tell her
what to do with them: temptation, this
spinning moon, these things I chase
through the dark, as if, all along,
I hadn't been awake at all.

Little Weeping Day With Trees Inside

When I'm out walking and the rain starts,
I mistake the sound, for a moment,
for my zippers softly bouncing
against my jacket, as I have this sort
of bounce to my walk,
a bounce my mother shared with me
just as when, once I'm full,
I slide my plate of food
across the table
making a sound like rain
inside the bowl on the table outdoors,
catching some and letting the rest go
down between the iron slats,
the spaces like sun coming in
between leaves and limbs
and getting all over me.
I read a letter from a friend
who can't stop writing about rain:
it sounds soft in the beginning
like someone walking around
a big empty house in a wedding dress,
as if loneliness were a sound
that keeps reminding me of myself,
quick and unthinking,
the way starlings
pull the leaves off my tomato plants.
And even though the starlings
have moved on, my plants are here and,
despite all the circumstances,
have pushed new leaves out
from their stems,
a miracle I wish I could catch
while weeding or on the porch
doing my flip-flap thing with the
bathroom rugs, unfolding in the sunshine
from these limb-stiff arms.

I'm growing spring-fat
under this red hair, redder there
where I've walked in the sun, and
I walk and I walk, but mostly I eat.
So I walk early
in the morning
where once a man was slumped in a chair
on his fine white porch,
more dead-looking than asleep,
his arm hanging,
his soft hand almost touching the porch floor gently
as birds, flying so close to our
architectures set like playthings among
their trees all talking in a language
we don't know yet.
And we think they're talking about us
because that's how we are,
always thinking about how we are.
So when I saw
the dead man I paused
in the same way
I pause for a passing car,
thinking only about myself—
What do I do? all I could think
beside the driveway that once held
a motorhome for sale, and it must have sold
because it was gone like the life from him
sometime in the night,
still there
hushing me
standing stupidly inside
a puddle of streetlamp light
and caught by the arm of the gracelessness
of not knowing what to do next,
a cage with no bars at all,
and the sleeping dead man

another interpretation
to sort through
with my fat fingers, my
little filing cabinets of choices
slid shut.
I keep walking,
bouncing along
like someone's mom in a wedding dress
with all my whispering zippers
pulled tight to the tops
of the trees where the starlings
look down at me with my tomato leaves
just hanging there lifeless,
reminding me of my place in all this:
how when I go home
to my room—where yesterday I was
crying over something
I've since forgotten—
I'll park myself inside on a chair,
square as a sold motorhome
puffing out the exhaust
I walk through which makes me cough
a tiny cough in my hand,
small and invisible just sitting there,
as something I remember
from a dream last night
flutters in and drops
its leaf into my day.
Just as I bend down to reach for it,
the wind,
just because she wanted to,
blows it all away.

Music of Hair

Day 3, the hospital water fountain,
not praying but drinking when
two ladies rounded the corner.
The little one with hair rising and falling
quiet as feathers, said to the other lady
(all our moments one moment),
the bus driver is praying for Jan.
And I, water from my chin,
but I am Jan, as if it were an argument,
as if I needed clarity (aren't I always needing clarity?),
and the little lady with hair sounding like cotton
said she was Jan, too, and, that, I guess,
means we're both covered, she said.
And I felt as close to her as if I were her,
myself in so many years with hair let go,
prayers let out from everyone as one.

Cut

I do not have my makeup on.
I remember I was 65 the first time
someone told me they loved me.
I remember the clouds.
I imagine what the sun would look like
to a blind man. I imagine too much
instead of being where I'm supposed to be.
I don't want to drown today,
but I might. I don't want to tell
everyone I love you, but I might.
Even though my husband knows,
he still reaches toward me.
What I heard him say was,
There's nothing you can do to make up
for what you've done.
I'm cold, I'm hot, I don't know.
I'm alone and counting flowers.
I'm alone and counting the cold coming.
The passing cars and all the people, their lives
no better or worse, just there passing.
I imagine all the wrong things
blowing around inside me like a storm,
like the woman, again, with no arms
watching her child swept away
by the rushing river.

Anesthesia

Leaves and petals attend me. I am ready.
— Sylvia Plath

For weeks it hasn't rained months
now all night I water the gardens
the fig tree the mosquitoes

holding hands laying me down
in the grasses not gently
quietly I cannot get up

I should have let the sun heal me
me with my tubes tied
around my neck and my daughter

watching horses watching clouds
only cartoon rain falling
asleep backwards into a hole

the nurse did nothing to keep me
here she seems not to like me
either I wake and I am nothing

look now how powerless I am
against drought against the bed
curtains and ceiling tiles

I feel their movement around me
but cannot see anyone
I do not want this to be

the nightmare I think it is
in the waiting room the ladies
file in each one as pregnant

as explosive everything pointed
toward me in the corner my ears
covered I hear them in there

screaming to get out they know
what I've done they are scared
there are no chairs left

no one calls for anyone
the only sound the secretaries
ringing telephones this room

their window they shut
behind curtains they've sewn
my lips closed because they know

the nurses who seemed at first
so friendly so quickly turned so
my friends and their effacement

look as clouds part as they pass
their hospital caps may never
rain they are tucking

me in tight and rolling me away
no one has told me where
my arms are strapped and my legs

we are rolling past windows now
each one a different day
different weather rain sun

burning so brightly the grasses
browning now around the terrible
flowers stretching hard toward the sun

my petals all aflame.

Patient # _____

> The sun shines down, and its image reflects in a thousand different pots filled with water. The reflections are many, but they are each reflecting the same sun. Similarly, when we come to know who we truly are, we will see ourselves in all people.
>
> —*Amma*

I went to the desert.
I fell in love
with an old horse.
His eyes softened
when I whispered to him.
I believe he loved me too.
But how will I ever know?
He turned back
as I latched the gate
for the last time.
And now I'm sad.
Now I wait,
fourth floor at the VA,
Mental Health.
The old man in the Vietnam cap
in nice neat shoes,
sits beside his wife as she
reads *Better Homes & Gardens*.
It occurs to me that many people
consider the waiting room a micro
version of what's going on
out in the streets.
There's a church sign out there.
I read it every day
on my way.
Blah, blah, blah,
just go to church,
it says.
There's a woman.
She can feel her higher power

from all her cells.
I want that.
I want my horse.
My daughter, not quite
catching on to the clear
channel of the radio,
calls the sound crusty.
I sometimes register
people as mere information
to pass.
I try to remember
to pray before I sleep
and again when I wake.
I pray for connection.
Some days I avoid
eye contact at all cost.
Some days all I eat for lunch
is raisins.
Someone in the hall
walks with a cane.
Last night my arm fell
asleep so heavily I felt
attached to a dead thing.
It was painful to feel it
come alive.
The receptionist in the window-
less space tapped her 15-year
trophy when I commented on
how often I see her.
My mother-in-law often
uses the phrase,
be still my heart.
The receptionist's heart
seems very still.
But how would I know?
Mine feels like a little bird

that likes to perch
at the tip of the limb.
At the restaurant the other day,
an old man complained about
the mashed potatoes: too lumpy.
His pants were pleated neatly.
I didn't see a wife anywhere.
Maybe she was too lumpy.
Sometimes I feel the dead thing
I'm attached to is my heart.
On my way to work,
I often pass the litter crew,
the prisoners in their stripes.
Each time, I imagine
slowing down to rescue them,
but then I remember
just how much I hate litter.

Or Dragons

From The Markey Cancer Center, Lexington, KY

My sponsor came to visit me at the hospital on Wednesday. We sat by
the fountain where she told me a story about lying in bed, unable
to fall asleep, and thinking of her two pairs of expensive shoes
outside on the porch. She was worried the neighborhood dogs
would come and chew them or she'd wake and find them full to
the laces with spiders. Or dragons. She woke in the morning and
found them, quiet as mice, beneath the bench. Clean, untouched.
Holy almost, as if our imaginations had made of them glorious
things that had, with all the grace of shoes, made it through
another night.

Sad, etc.

The sunlight, the warmth
on the roof.
The snow slides off.
My father ducks.
Some old bomb detonating
at last or again
through the roof.
I lean over him but nothing,
just the quietness of his
bald head, a few gray hairs
holding on—
the legs of a butterfly
climbing the flower stem—
soft, neighborly,
and ours, looking,
always looking at us
from their tiny windows.
And I am in a tank top again,
spring planting again,
hoping the flowers
will hold on
again, my father
petting the dog there,
recalling again
the blackness
behind his heart attack—
proof in the nothingness
beyond.
His hands, sliding down
the dog, two runways
to the heart.
I dig and dig,
and the dirt smells
kind of nice.

After Running to My Daughter Late in the Night, She Tells Me Her Nightmare Is About Snakes, Not Poisonous, and a Little Bit of Bears

I do not know if people like
to give statistics about
Deaths in America or if it's
a habit or if it makes them feel
certain about something or other,
but I do not like it. Especially
when my daughter in the next room
is meowing or when an airplane
is flying over our house, and I think
of my brother, a new pilot.
He gave me a ride in his plane
once, told me to hold the yoke.
My hands turned to water.
Here, right down here, in the yard
next to the bird bath, with a
handsaw under the cherry blossoms,
I'm sawing and I'm strong.
But the winter, and the things
people say. But the garden
and the scattered seeds.
My hunger and my husband
at the grill. My daughter's
nightmares are still cute.
The birds do not believe her
meows, or, in an air of grilling
chicken, they do not believe
they are next. If I were always
thinking about distances instead
of fear, I'd say how, from the ground,
the plane looks like a toy or how,

when I was flying with my brother,
the whole world seemed tender,
and I was just floating along,
simple as a cloud, my only job
for the day to fill the birdbath
and watch the birds go wild.

Shiloh

Our house went on the market today.
A lady wants to come take a look.
So I am here with nowhere else to go,
with the dog, just sitting
in this space—the church,
the rows of gravestones.
All morning I spent on my hands and knees.
Soon she'll see how magnificently
my floors shine, my legs now, too, in the sun,
mirrors and the wind.
The flap to my dress is flapping.
When I close my eyes, the wheat sounds
like waves. I am at the beach of the dead.
What washes up: the dog in the shadow
of my chair. My bra strap shows a little bit.
It is hot; I'm rolling my clothes in tight
toward my heart. The bones of the dead
are in very neat rows. I washed my hair
in the sink this morning, hung my towel
on the bare hook. Why can't I be
holy and exquisite like the dead?
I hear somewhere a tractor.
I hear somewhere myself but older,
reaching backwards with
forgiveness in her eyes.
The metal roof of the old church cracks.
Clouds pinch by.
My empty cup tries to catch in the wind.
We are moving soon to another state.
Every single thing is about to change.
If I could stay right here, I'd spend all my days
documenting the slow growth and diminishment
of the house shadows.
Be quiet, be quiet, I'd say,
my hair is trying to sleep.

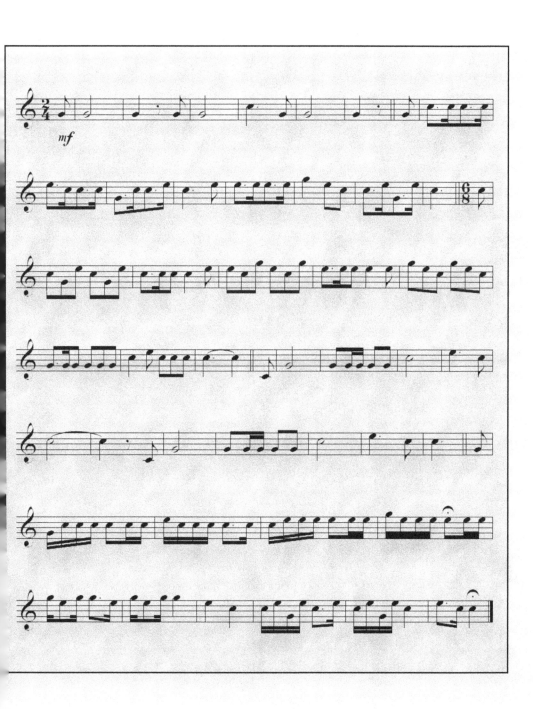

The Sound Off

After Christine Blasey Ford's testimony to the
Senate Judiciary Committee

In Requiem for the Living, the father explains to his daughter,
If I am calm
it is because I have spent most of a lifetime
learning to live with myself, which is the hardest
marriage of all.

My friend K in Tennessee writes back to me thick letters.
In bed last night (where I was alone, my husband and daughter gone for
      the weekend),
I read from her: Even when you talk about feeling crazy, your letters
are so calm, serene.
I feel like I'm floating through your pretty world with the sound on
      mute.
J used to watch TV that way,
with the sound off.

There's this thing in the Army
called: "Sound Off,"
which means to holler, make noise.
But I hardly do—I lip-sync.
My enthusiasm has nothing to do with my voice.

My letters don't seem to be communicating my anxious grappling
      toward
      some thing
      some thing
      some thing.

Only when I'm alone
do I feel this house properly
or accurately.
The creaks of the floorboards.

When I lived alone, a decade ago,
I fell in love with my house—
    my upstairs apartment.

I like our dog better when it's
        just me and him.
His sweet wag. His small life
depends on me now. His dry food in the bowl.
How the nuggets roll
off the scoop reminds me
I've been buried alive by noise—
TV, sirens, phones—my internal voice, she's been yelling.

My daughter on the way to school walked into
a spider's web and let out a scream
that may have woken the world
as it lay sleeping around
me now. The early morning.
The whirr of the washing machine.

      On our group run
this morning, we talked of laundry,
the rituals of husbands
    with theirs,
      wives with theirs.
My husband and daughter away
    and I'm here, folding
      their socks.

My book on tape: the lady tells me
we don't live fully in ourselves.
We live from the head up.

I haven't been living in my socks. Neither the cotton ones nor the
    wool.

She also said, Every thought is connected to a sensation in the body.

I was alone at work yesterday
so I tried to practice this—
    thinking, then feeling
all these roots winding around
inside me. The noise. The search for sensation.

On the run it was dark—
    I looked up at the sky to the stars and felt
connected to them and open.
My body felt so capable.
A second later, the men began talking about some big thing
on the news that everyone in the group had something to say about.
                I felt a cord in
                my hip tighten
    like something in me was
                wearing down
    on another something.
                    My heart, I guess.

My daughter glues eyes to pompoms.
    They sit on the sill and look
        at me—
    I do not know what it is
        they are seeing in me.
Their pupils go every which way.

Every morning, because I work on an army base,
I have to go through the gate.
When the arms of the gate go up, they seem
so open, accepting.
There's this one gate guard (there are four to six entrances, depending
    on time of day)
    who never smiles.
    I always take it personally.
My internal voice snaps into
        this image of him
grumpily disregarding me,
looking down at me from his perch.

I gave my coworker a
    sticky note
that said, Tomorrow will be better,
and she keeps it on her desk.
        What I meant was: It can be better now.
I don't want to wait for
            tomorrow;
    nor do I want her to wait.
I've seen her heart; she's told me things.
        (I'm so busy trying to read my own heart.)

I'm trying to visualize flowers growing
    behind me where I've stepped.
In a book on tape I learned this.
        I am a receptacle for
    good advice and dirty looks.
I'm shaking them up.

On our run this morning, R said T (who wasn't there) used to take
so many pills and vitamins before their runs, powder would come
from his mouth by the third mile.
We were on mile five and I'd never
    felt as thirsty as I had
        in that second.

My friend R asked me yesterday
about that political thing
(the one the runners were talking about this morning)
and I asked him if he'd ever
crapped on the side of the road during
one of his long runs.
Maybe that's the image
that I come to—or the sensation
of my body connected to the thoughts
of all I don't know/can't understand.
Maybe I'm focusing too much
    on the ends instead of
what is in between.
        I think I may treat
my marriage like this.

The top and the bottom.
The beginning and the end.
I'm always making suggestions
        about The End.
Wanting to stop the noise of
    marriage.
Like a strong wind I've been
standing out in.
        The sand in my eyes.
It's a desert wind, I guess.

    Last night, after I opened
all the doors and windows of this house
(that today I'm falling in love with)
my neighbor texted,
        There's a criminal on
                the loose.
Fear: she always finds me.

I'm a woman—I have
considered breast implants (this is a confession).
But I feel like I'd be carrying
around a couple of visitors.
Like how I dream of ghosts.
    And always the next day
I wonder: Is the ghost my subconscious?
        My husband?
        My spirit guide? (My palm reader in Tennessee said I have one.)
        Myself from years ago?
        Myself from a life
                I've wanted—
one where every day is
                just this quiet.

    I went to the city and in
        a shop was a
needlepoint of a flower pot.

Beside the pot it said,
        I'm sorry.
It made me want to take up needlepoint.
This morning I thought about
    crocheting again as I do
when the fall comes on.

    The tree out front just
turned to me with her orange leaves,
        but I could not hear her,
or was that my heart?

I'm sorry, everyone.

Lamplight, 6 p.m.

My husband and I are on a date
like all couples everywhere, I guess.
But the restaurants, they're all filled,
waiting lines out the doors and up the streets.
The couples everywhere flocking under streetlights——
the darkness an arm's length away and holding.
So he has this idea, my husband—the hotel restaurant.
The one with the pool he spent the weekend swimming in
with his sister and her family last year while we were separated.
When I was trying to find myself,
stepping into the darkness fully.
I navigate the dark hallways of this new house,
an old house, midnight, my hand along the wall,
to the bathroom, the nightlight over the sink
pretty and soft. I step into it now.
My husband told me the pool water was freezing.
And how he swam, back and forth, back and forth.
We press our hands and faces against the windows to look.
The pool lights shining up from the pool floor,
bending in all directions.
In all that water, in all that light, he could not find me.

Drowning Boy

When my boss was having a heart attack and the big
male nurse above her was doing all he could with CPR,
people everywhere in the hospital were praying, she said,
the prayers rising up or drifting down across all four floors.
I wonder about prayer, the prayer we say at dinner each night:
Thank you God for food so good, help us do the things we should.
Where that prayer heads to, off over our glasses, I don't know,
but it seems important to remind ourselves to be good.
When my daughter comes at me with questions, like when
she asked me what slavery is (or was?), I was glad the shower
curtain hung between us. The confessional. The father,
the son. I read they kept a black woman locked in a room
for years for their own pleasure. The iron on the ankle,
the chains. I can't look in the mirror. I scrub my daughter's hair
with soap that smells like honey and makes the house smell
so sweet. That is what I begin with when I tell her, Honey.
Honey, there was this man. Honey, my hair is so quickly
turning gray. My hairdresser says it's an evolutionary process
to show a person is losing their fertility. I believe everything
my hairdresser tells me. My friend believes it was prayer
that saved her, not the heart doctor who happened to be
an atheist; he climbed two floors to her and found the blood
clot that was killing her. Do you ever really know what is killing you?
My husband told me how a little boy in Texas survived the floods
by using his dead mother as a raft. Once, at a waterpark
up the road, we were drifting down the lazy river when I saw a boy
bobbing up-down, up and down, and every time he came up,
Daddy, he'd say, quiet as water, and I ran to him and lifted him,
his bones all sticks. The lifeguard asked if he was mine. I said
yes. I think I rose out of the water then, giant and winged,
gathering all the children around me, mothers, fathers, even
the lifeguards high in their chairs though they were scared.

Some things happen too quickly to notice. When I was driving
to work the other day, I passed a man on a bicycle, a BMX.
He was riding fast and wild, a guitar on his back that I'm sure
was heavier than he was, his hair only sprouts. He looked
beautiful and free, but when I passed I saw it, his face dripping
with blood so red and fresh, the celebration I had been
feeling for him so quickly slipped into fear for my own life,
how to protect myself against some sort of violence that seems
to be hiding right there, behind everything. If he had been a boy.
Or a dog. Or a woman in a room with her legs falling open.
I haven't a prayer for this. Dinner with the fork right there
on the napkin. I'm not the only one who imagines what I'll look like
when I'm dead. Lately, the sky refuses to rain, and the whole
world has turned brown. When I pass the graveyards on my drive
to work, I imagine the dirt around the coffins there receding
and the boxes with the bodies falling deeper away from us.
In an essay on enlightenment I read this: At the cellular level, it's evident
the fundamental nature of life is a desire to expand, which makes
me wonder how much of myself I've been living in, what
percentage, what fraction, what part of me is already dying.
Tonight, perhaps, we'll say a better prayer, something expansive
that'll include all this and everything. When I tell my husband
I want to be more like the flowers, like the grasses, all these things
that are fighting to live right to the edges of themselves, he reminds
me of the poisonous vines, the kudzu. Look around, he says. Even
the oleander, as pretty as it is. So I tell him, Let's pray for them too.

Before Bed My Husband Called Me an Old Testament God

While we slept, the whole town turned
to ice. A tree fell on the garage
in the middle of the night.
We woke and ran to the window,
but it was too dark to see.
In the morning we drove slowly
across the ice-covered roads.
In the back seat, my little girl, with the saddest voice,
asked about the trees falling on the cows.
All the cows are safe in the barns, I said, but
she knew. I just saw five, she said, and I had seen them too.
We drove slowly, each of us pointing
to all the fallen things; the world, it seemed,
in ruins, and as a deer ran quickly across
the road in front of us, I had to remind myself
that all of this was not my fault.

How To Give Credit

The day the musk deer dies, he falls
to the ground, his horn punctures
his stomach, and what escapes
is the beautiful scent he spent
his life searching for. I'm thinking
of this when my uncle calls,
when he tells me my grandfather said
he is ready to die, and he's going
to take his little black dog with him.
Sometimes when I swim in the pool
at lunch I pretend my worries
are washing off and falling like
river silt to the bottom.
Sometimes my coworker comes
with me and just stands there
in the middle of the lane we share,
and I pass her, lap after lap.
I catch a glimpse of her on an in-breath,
there smiling, in her swim cap and goggles,
her nose pinched with a clip.
She tries to tickle my foot as I pass, but I'm
serious about my swim. I keep going,
my laugh half submerged
which I imagine sounds like
the quick sound of a loud room
right before the door is shut.
Like how my daughter and I opened
the car door at Cumberland Falls a few
weeks ago and heard for the first time
the great sound of the river falling.
We stood on the concrete platforms

below the falls, by the side of the falls,
at the top of the falls, where my daughter
and her little friend threw sticks into
the river and watched them catch
and disappear over the edge. Each time
they would holler, That's my stick,
as if it were a magnificent accomplishment,
and I think, no matter how often the world
replays the ends, I still can't get used to them.

Roots

Once I saw my shadow in water, and glanced back,
but I was gone.
                                        —*Larry Levis*

And those hours out on the road alone
running until I cannot stop. I know

what will grow beneath my feet. I've seen
the weeds turn thick as trees.

I've seen the shadow of my heart
straining against this burning.

Iron pumping my legs belong to something
other, some other body is sleep.

Straining in the dark reminds me
of dying and dying. Once,

a man took me while I was asleep
and am I only now telling you

how I miss the pain of longing
for the road, for the sense of knowing

how to go and just going, but I have to
sit still now with my bones and heart all wrong,

like I've put them down somewhere
and cannot remember where or which way

is right, and somewhere my grandmother
is forgetting sugar in her pie, so what?

So I'm glad that someday I'll spend half a day
looking for my shoes and the other

half wondering if I should put my feet
in them, or by then will I have crossed

you out like that game my girl taught me to play?
Birds, they skitter from weed to weed

like hearts with feathers, she says, with no
body or bones or reason left to stay.

Somewhere

Early spring and only the crocuses,
morning and my work shirt, the one
with daisies. Grasses so real that when I stood
over my daughter to wake her, in her half-dream
I grew, a cloud of wildflowers she reached for.
She came away with nothing, and I've been away,
too many hotel breakfasts, too many people
waiting for their waffles—I can barely see them,
my Styrofoam plate too thin to hold what I need.
I am only one, standing in line behind the others,
looking down. I hold hands with my daughter
as we walk. I do not know if it is my sweat
or hers between us, a little pool, an ecosystem—
what is growing there? What am I letting
seep into her? In the shower, she pulls
at her nipples. When will I become a woman,
she asks, the look on her face so far from me.
Today I met a soldier who once drove over
a little girl the size of his own. He had to,
to save himself, to save a hundred others.
My daughter today will stand on the edge
of the high dive even though I warned her,
and then she'll jump. The clouds reflected there
will pass beneath all those faces in the pool
like moons looking up through the branches
I stand beneath, where I holler, I am no longer
afraid of you, and I believe it because I have to.

I Dreamed I Was Riding
Through Water on a Dead Galloping Horse

I am alone in the house and had been wishing
for this aloneness, but now I'm lonely.
I'm writing another letter to a friend telling her,
When I feel I'm resisting what is,
I sing a little bit, which may have been
a lie, which letters, like art, are sometimes guilty of.
I wake from a dream and look out across
the bed to the clock, my husband gone,
the bed expansive, the blue comforter
pooling beside me. I pull up for a breath.
I find myself in the morning
in prayer, in letters, in a psalm I read
to the dog with his bone, to the sweet
dishwasher churning (I must be lonely),
...and the little hills rejoice on every side.
I write about the hike along the river with a new friend.
How we came upon a big rock where a family of wild
teenaged boys were performing flips off the side—off
into the shallow waters.

Let's jump, she said, as if that were
a choice. I stood shaking on the rock's edge,
my old bones rattling like the old bones
in "The Witch of Coos," the wild ones that stood
halting perplexed behind the barrier of door and headboard,
the ones that shook like a pile of dishes.
Jump, she said, and then the lady
sunbathing on the shore chimed in,
and the bikers along the path and the swimmers below,
all the voices orchestrating my fear—a hundred noisy bells
until   ker-plunk, like a cartoon I did it.

What's more, all the characters in this moment of my life—
men with hair down their backs and wild faces I will never see again—
coerced me next to swing from the rope.
And I did though I was frightened and rattling again,
and I think and write about this now, days later, with sore shoulders,
my legs sore, oh but my heart and the memory of this jumping—
I can hear those hills singing right now.
It is hard to believe it happened at all
from where I stand, over the dishes in the washer shaking,
spooning sorghum onto leftover cornbread,
which I, alone, carried home last night in a little napkin
across the parking lot.
The butternut squash roasts for the bread I'll bake.
I make the bed, stand between headboard
and door, floating through dark and quiet.

Yellow

When I lived in the barracks at Fort Campbell,
there was this private, Chen, who had Tourettes.

We'd be standing in formation, all of us, so straight
and tall, and he'd be back there, two ranks away, saying

fuck, shit, fuck, shit, and I, a private too, would have to
knock out twenty push-ups because I'd be laughing

and laughing, there with my boots on the line, and then
we'd march off to breakfast just like that, as if we weren't

all so lonely, as if the sun wasn't burning our eyes.
The birds and the bullets, butter melting on the grits.

When I used to deliver mail on a rural route, there was
this man on Katherine Street who always wanted me

to go to the barn with him, to look at the baby chicks.
One day, I was so lonely I walked with him,

this strange man, right into this barn alone on a hill,
and he set his arms over the wooden gate as if to take

some great weight off, but there was nothing there,
just some old rotting hay bales and slats of sun coming in

through slats of old wood around us, and what, again,
had I gotten myself into? What kind of epidemic is it

the Surgeon General has declared on us, how loneliness
is killing us faster than 15 cigarettes a day? I believe

it's because my husband left the closet door open one night,
that neither one of us could sleep. We tossed and turned

like two burning logs rolling away from each other,
each repelled by the heat of the other, our easy lives

made difficult by our hearts, and our hearts and the roads
running out in all directions, and my life, according to

the palm reader across town, is going to be a long one.
There'll be children there laughing, a little boy, she said.

I stand here and I call to him from all of my chakras,
because the palm reader, she said, too, that my yellow one

below my ribs is dying, fading like the sun over the horizon
I'm driving toward and there's this singer on the radio

who, when she talks, has a stutter, but her singing voice
is beautiful. It sounds yellow, like butter

melting over my white white heart. She makes me feel
like I'm not the only one in the world dying from this.

For the Curtains and the Wind in the Curtains

Every year I dress as the angel of death.
Except this year, I am a fallen angel.
I made it, with everyone I know,
door to door, a hundred houses down
to the bottom with our candy buckets.
Time, as with ghosts, is a sheet with eyeholes
spreading in all directions. Inflatable
dinosaurs standing in line. You know,
I've knocked on a million doors and cannot
tell who is real. My daughter, at seven, walking in heels,
both child and lady at once, right now beside me.
Leaves and grasses glued to my shirtsleeves.
I'm trying to make it to the next door before
this feeling of being buried alive already, once
familiar, returns. Jesus, I say, the babies
at the bottom of the hill all crying at once.
Bedtime, as they know it, has passed
though they are awake; their chocolates
for some other time. Time as something other, okay?
Look, her boot heel's stuck in the lawn, and they
are all too tired to go on. So I'll carry you,
I say to the children, the babies, the mothers with
sore hips. Even outside of war a test of strength, or
strength is all I can believe in to get up this hill tonight.
Or are we up there already, the ghosts behind us
staring at our backsides through their eyeholes?
I can carry more, even with a hundred
plastic pumpkins bumping against
my shoulder blades. And, oh Jesus,
my knees, my necklace of twigs and branches.
I am prehistoric. I am doing this
holiday trick of being dead and alive,
of believing and not at once.

Hallelujah

> I can't keep track of the track there's nothing but
> side trails of love and sadness...
> —*Alice Notley*

Mid-March: I don't want to hear any more
about winter.
Shhh.
You don't either,
do you?
Do you?
Which who?
In a letter to K:

Winter has found her quiet way inside me.

Grocery store flowers right through kitchen countertops, windowsills,
    table.
My little girl and her turtle and owl, their little stone eyes; me, my
    blank eyes
and the Virgen de Guadalupe, her wick-fire heart.
So I haven't been a virgin for a hundred years or more. Everyone knows
    it.

I know what I've been doing.
My brother on the telephone tells me about the Snowflake Parade:
Children froze to their instruments:
one girl, one clarinet,
together forever, hallelujah.

Love doesn't.
Forever scares me to pieces.
Okay, so when I snap the branch of my marriage, out
come a hundred men marching.

I'm a soldier at attention with
averted eyes and wind in my heart.

It's a simple matter of energy transfer or
the Wild West of my heart,
doors kicked open,
guns I am running from, these holes
in me bleeding, unfillable yet
I can't remember who I'm in love with, or why.

When I asked the tattoo artist to tattoo the wind on me,
he asked where. Now it is sorrow: I'm tied to
this affliction, so there's church. Oh no, I'm
in love with Jesus or fear or everyone in between.
I keep coming back.

I tuck my shirt into my pants, into
the cuff bottoms of my white-sock heart,
my wick-fire heart,
my heart my heart my heart:
Are you sick of me yet?
Every one and everyone at the same time,
yet I don't miss anyonething
not even the blackness in between.

In how many ways did I disappoint my daughter today?
This could be what all this is about.

I don't want to play in the snow, thank you.
I move from window to window looking out
at her pointing to her little snowmen:

Men,
all of them
small as hands,
one on the bench, others under the tree, on the trash can, along the fence,

their little rock eyes looking
at my little rock eyes inside.

My hand on the vacuum or my heart windows and my daughter there:
I need to save her from me, quick.

Dragon

Our neighbors are so close and looking,
always looking, and here I am
in a tank top again, no bra, shoveling
poop again and crying about a little girl
who is my little girl's friend.
The little girl fell from the Ferris wheel.
I search the news frantically, but
nothing. I've been crying and my eyes
hurt, the sunlight hurts, and the neighbors
won't stop looking at me, and my wave
is dumb and heavy. I want to put
my arms to bed again like the old dogs
they are. The little girl who fell
from the Ferris wheel rode the little dragon
roller coaster with my little girl
a few minutes before she fell.
I have a friend who does not have
children. I do not want to see her today.
I'm in the yard hanging my little girl's
shirt from the line, the one, you know,
with the glow-in-the-dark bones.
The shirt's so old the bones are peeling
off, and I try to pretend my fear is a wall
that can protect her. But it's nothing,
just a wall between me and some sort
of joy I can see from here. I can almost
wave to it, but my arms are heavy, too heavy,
today. I am scary with these eyes.
My little girl, who asked me three times
to ride the Ferris wheel. Her face shining
up at me, bright as a sunflower, okay?

And that's how the two of them looked,
one behind the other in the seats
of the dragon. She asked me, Please,
please? as the helicopters above us
hauled the bodies away. When I drive
across town, I can see the Ferris wheel
rising up like some terrible mistake.
Who am I to go to the store today,
to buy milk today, when the flowers
are here and the neighbors are watching,
and everything and everyone is looking
at me like I'm supposed to know what to do—

Egg Harbor and My Orphan Heart

The horse barn I wait in for my daughter
is always so cold.
I bring a blanket, one my mother-in-law
crocheted, one I kept when
my husband took half of everything
and moved down the street.
Beyond the barn, the field is split
between sunlight and darkness.
Just beyond that beyond
is a well, and I, on the shore,
fill everything with—what shall I call it?—
grief?
My old, old house,
my husband's, even older.
My fear of burning to death in my sleep—
not unreasonable at all, but my chairs are.
Three of the four break under
the weight of the husband.
So I went to the shore and said goodnight
to the ocean; I went to the shore and said,
I'm sorry. When my daughter gathers
her toy horses for the bath,
the winged and the wingless, she lines them up
on the tub's shore and sings and sings.
I am more chair today than anything else.
I am more burning than anything else.
When my girl rises from the bath,
steaming like something pulled from
a fire, I tell her, Your voice, it's so lovely.
It wasn't me, she says.
It was my horses.

Like Dust Motes in a Sunbeam

How strange and nice it was
to run into my husband
at the grocery store.
I was there buying half-and-half;
he was there buying chips.
We had just left the house
separately. We'd been fighting—
we felt like strangers meeting there,
as if we'd just flashed into our lives
years from now. All the shelves
neatly stacked around our mess.
The automatic glass doors shut
between us, just before
our conversation was over.

1984 to Now

The stars are not wanted now: put out every one.
                    —*W. H. Auden*

I slow down on the road, my daughter in the back seat,
so the two of us can watch a pair of vultures pull apart that little pile
of something that had been something else not long ago

not far from making it to the other side, and I think about what I read
recently, that the essential characteristic of death is that it gives advance warning
of its arrival, but this is too obvious. Kid, I say, let's just use this

as an after school lesson. 'Tis the season anyway. I drive around the scene
so she can explain why it is impossible to tell what the road kill had been
as her new earrings catch the sun, the rearview, my eyes. And I was 7, too,

when mine were pierced. It was the day they caught the Beauty Queen Killer,
April 13, 1984. He was trying to make it to Canada. He'd made it all the way to us,
to our small town in northern New Hampshire where I stood on the street

with everyone I knew. Almost there, I whispered. What is it we all have in common?
Hope? Death? How many beauties had he killed on his stretch from Florida
to New Hampshire? You can look it up. Almost there. The cat in the road,

if it had been a cat, a killer, too. My daughter, dammit, is too pretty. Real diamonds
in her ears. Look at her, he said. I've been listening my entire life. I've been running.
When we get home, the kid runs full blast to the scarecrow, the one we made

last weekend, with bugs crawling from its eyes, the one that stares
all night at the streetlamp—his stare so dark the light bursts, and my heart.
I watch my daughter lean in to his pumpkin cheek for a kiss.

Lamplight, 8:30 p.m.

After our date, we pick up our daughter at the church.
All the ladies there, I could not tell what they were smiling about.
Their shirts said, Be the light! Be the light! Be the light!
Sometimes I close my eyes and try to expel some part of me
I'm not sure I even see. It's like how I understand
stars feel fighting through darkness.
It was so bright in the church, the church café
glistening, the ladies glistening,
and I saw her, my daughter, across the room,
so tired, her little eyes:
below them, little suitcases of tired.
The suitcases in the basement want to be filled,
want to go somewhere, anywhere, really.
I keep thinking we will, but there's always an excuse—
a new job, a new house, two houses, old houses,
a new cancer in an old organ.
A blizzard, a town I can't get into for all the snow.
So when my uncle dies, the week before Valentine's,
I can only make phone calls, send condolence cards I keep
forgetting to mail no matter which table I pile them on.

Tomorrow is President's Day.
I told my running friends after we ran
in the dark, 600 degrees below zero,
across a parking lot punctuated by lamplights,
Remember the presidents!
I have no idea what I meant by this.
Then last night, as if my dream with her little hands
reached down into the light and pulled this thing out,
I was on the committee to write the Declaration of Independence!
My husband would laugh at this if I remember to tell him.
He might say, Now that's something.

In the dream, my nose was running fast and heavy
like a sink faucet or a waterfall over glistening rocks,
and like a dream tugging on a memory, there we were,
waiting for the moonbow.
We were tourists with camera phones.
I stood inside a millisecond flash,
my eyes closed to the brightness.
Then I fell like water back into the dark.
I had to navigate my way out, my hand against the cold rock.

Seven-and-a-Half-Minute Mile

Some nights, before all this, I'd lie awake
and think about the tulips, the ones
I didn't get to see this year. I knew it even then,
there, next to my husband. I'd shiver all night,
20 pounds lost and I felt naked. I'd say, I'm freezing
to death. Of course I'd say that, but the death was some
other type of closing, something I had been holding
for forty years. But today, I just want a tuna melt.
Today, I walked to work more slowly than I usually do,
looked at the roses longer, breathed in longer.
Today is my last day at work. While I hung clothes
on the line this morning, I told my daughter to say
good morning to the flowers. They're everywhere
this spring. They're here as if they're making up
for something. Winter's a little sorry.
When I opened the door to my body, all my organs
flew out and around like wild birds, but they came back,
as I am their resting place. My daughter laughed
when the llama said good night to the tree shadow.
When my husband pulled a handful of broken
cupboard latches from his pocket, I thought of
my thoughts, if that makes any sense to you.
It's okay, I once drew a picture of the cabin of
an airplane, and the perspective made me realize
I'll never quite understand the space I'm in.
I forgot to tell you, the mile I ran in the rain,
it was the fastest I'd run in 20 years.
Getting older really means getting better
at some things, I guess, while my body
busily keeps me humble about it.
The only thing I'll miss about this job is how
the hand dryers in the bathroom make the skin
of my hands flap so loudly. Sometimes I close
my eyes and pretend I am holding little motorcycles,
but I'll be alright, don't you worry.

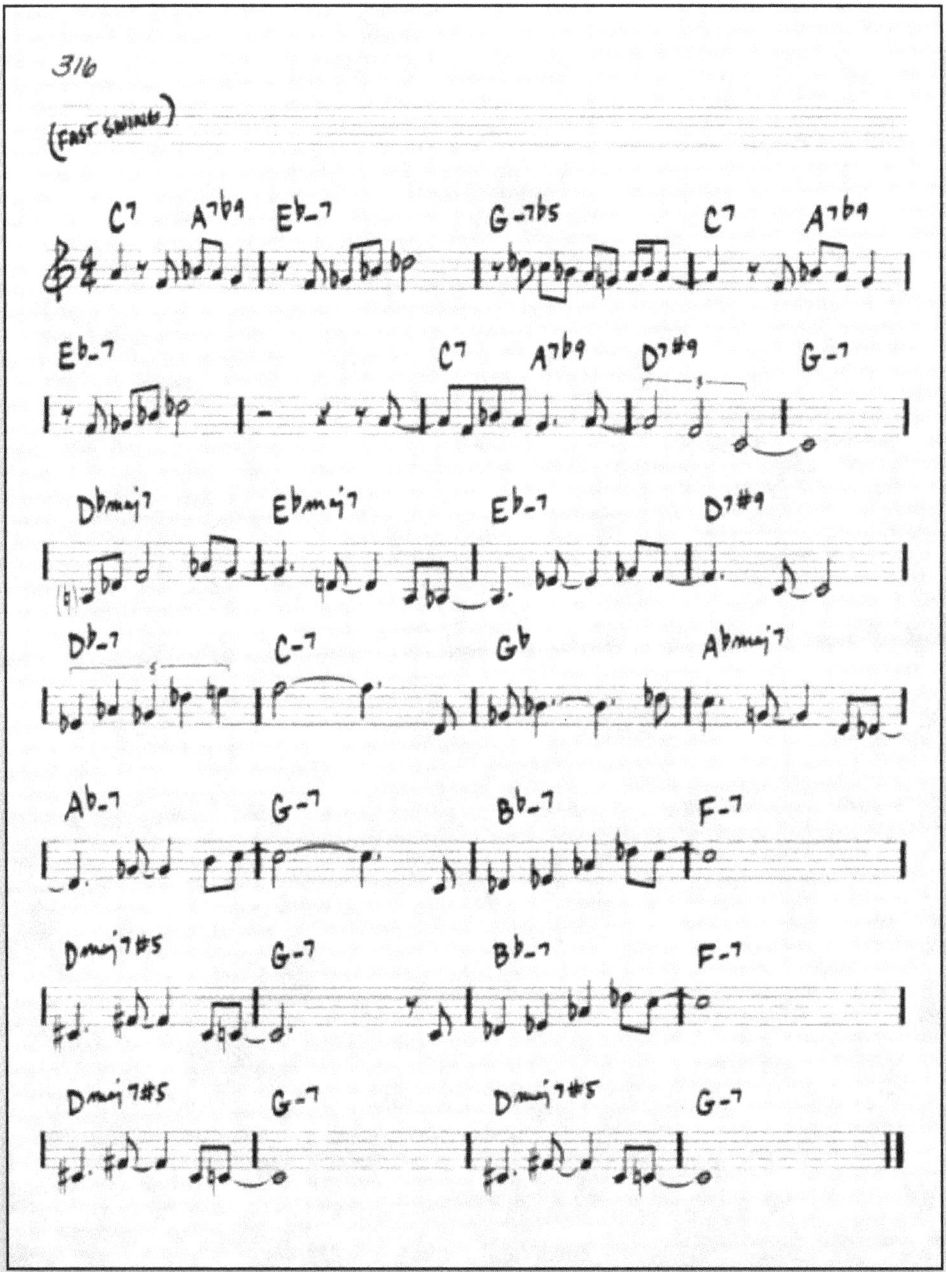
316
(FAST SWING)
C7 A7b9 Eb-7 G-7b5 C7 A7b9
Eb-7 C7 A7b9 D7#9 G-7
Dbmaj7 Ebmaj7 Eb-7 D7#9
Db-7 C-7 Gb Abmaj7
Ab-7 G-7 Bb-7 F-7
Dmaj7#5 G-7 Bb-7 F-7
Dmaj7#5 G-7 Dmaj7#5 G-7

Wallpaper

My husband right now is standing on the rim
of the tub, painting walls from which yesterday
he peeled layers of wallpaper, one layer, old roses;
another, images of change purses and handkerchiefs
like the one I wear around my nose and mouth to keep the mold out.
My job is to sweep the torn pieces of paper that cover the sink, tub,
and floor. My husband doesn't wear a handkerchief, doesn't wear
a mask, my husband who will be pumped through with chemo again on Monday.
I've told my friend in a letter how we flow through this quiet rhythm of sickness
and recovery weekly, like this is all sort of pretty, like we're really just
vacationing. Look, we've got our boat, we've our river, not even a cloud in the sky.
Look, it's nice to have nowhere to go.
It's just us and the trees there to tell us, be still, be still,
right? Isn't that the lesson? Be still and know, it says in the bathroom
at church. I try to be funny when I say the toilet paper understands.
Funny is weirder, these days. We play it cool and invite friends over.
They have a three-year-old boy. Before they come, we discuss whether
he is more like a tornado or a hurricane. At dinner, when he disappears
around the corner, my husband and I cringe. We are so tense, we can hardly
keep the conversation going, each of us privately
but together as we wait to hear a glass break, or a plate—
a feeling that never really leaves us.

Dear Tuth Fary

This is the beginning of my
daughter's letter, and in its folds
a tiny tooth, small as the foot of the mouse
we caught this morning in a trap
that looks like a hallway to heaven.
The light at the end illuminating a dollop
of peanut butter, heaven enough
for the mouse who was still alive,
still zipping its stringy tail back and forth
across the hardwood. My daughter
and I went outside to set it free, left the tea
warm on the counter, the teabag
with one of those little paper sayings,
The earth laughs in flowers, but there's no laughing here,
just ice creeping across everything, making us feel
even more zippered-in, my daughter
on the threshold right before the cry.
She could go either way, and this is always
up to me to maneuver. So I make up some life
for this mouse to get back to, some little car,
tiny house, little teacup tinier than a mouse tooth.
Isn't it all so cute? Isn't it great, how I can
hold the world in the light like this?
I cannot talk to her about why the mouse
went in there, the temptation, peanut butter
and loneliness, the pinhole of light in all the darkness,
like when she woke in the middle of the night
and came to my door to say, so sweetly, Hi mama,
which I snuffed out quickly with all my middle-aged
darkness. Midnight breath its own nightmare.
In the morning, I go to my coffee, my office
in the attic where I belong, and the squirrels

scrabble across the shingles and we laugh a little,
we being me and the comic part of me that
pops her head through the skylight to talk
to the critters above and below, and I can hear
it all from there. The inconsequential-ness
of my life is a cinch on my heart. The sweetness, too,
of my little girl growing into the most beautiful person
I have ever seen. That's enough.
The dark and the light are neck and neck again.
I am freezing from my heart up.
I am right here, rooting from the window.

Bright Red Morning

Late January, 22 degrees, and spitting snow.
So when my running friends ask if I'll be there
at 5 am like we are every Wednesday, I say, Ha Ha.
Ha Ha? My next question for the nurse after I ask her
if we could take my husband's organs home
for a broth. Ha Ha! I yell in my head when she writes something
down on her clipboard. The room not-funny quiet,
and I hope this moment doesn't determine some future
treatment for him, and I keep talking. I tell the nurse
about my friend who owns a crematorium.
It's all I can think of. I tell her how some lady called my friend
and asked if she could cremate her finger, wear it in a necklace,
but that just digs the hole deeper and there's a new
special kind of quiet in the room with the nurse and my husband,
who's looking at me with his be-quiet face, our fears turned inside out
a hundred times until the rims of them are sore. And I don't
ever really know what to say so I usually just stay quiet.
And I wish the hospital room was one of those times.
But I was so uncomfortable, and my husband had this tube
that ran out his nose and was pulsing green stomach stuff.
And he kept looking down at it for days. And when the blood came pulsing through,
I stood in the hallway with my sleep hair and hospital socks that I had taken
from his pile of new ones, and I was quiet when I shouldn't have been.
The hallways were so shiny and the wall art nice enough that I had taken pictures of it,
just staring at me stupidly. And the lady with the finger—or I mean without the finger—
was having trouble finding the finger, and that's all I could think about
in the hallway when I didn't know what to do or who to yell for. So I don't even know
if she's somewhere wearing it around her neck. But I wonder sometimes when I see
someone with a big necklace, and my daughter wondered when my friend
showed up in her crematorium truck with CREMATORIUM on the side,
with a bag of chicken for us because we had just gotten back from the hospital.
And she's a good friend, and my daughter at the window sounding it out,

CRE-MA-TOR-IUM, and the chicken from KFC so I knew it'd be good.

And I held the mashed potatoes under my daughter's nose, hoping she'd forget the truck

for a minute because I was hospital tired, and I still had my hospital socks on,

and my daughter likes them, how they feel like those little pads under our rugs

that keep them in place. And I feel like the socks are doing that for me,

keeping me here, keeping me from running as fast as I can into the bright red morning.

From Now On, Yes I Will

I went outside for a little sunshine, and I left you
there on the couch, coloring and cartoons. I wanted my own pretty.

A walk with the dog and the man next door yelling from the lip
of his sagging house—this turbid language there must be an answer.

I look for someone or something and only the shifting
of a plastic bag, billowing and lifting. Down the road a little,

another man with a look like the-more-you-say-no
the-harder-he'll-push. I know you're kind; I know you're kind—

my tight little incantation. I try but look where above him hangs
low a basket of fabric flowers, brown as if they'd just

pushed up through the roof of his grave, and I see
a woman there too, big and tired-like, half in and out of her car.

Her cigarette, her tailpipe. There's nowhere she can get to
to be where you are. I keep it okay and I'm sorry

I'm doing nothing more than telling you nothing
to keep this simple. The eyes of these houses are closed,

and the eyes looking out are empty. Please, sir, don't hurt me and
my little dog; look how softly we are aging together, right here,

right now. I've too many ends left dangling. I'm shivering
against the branches. I'm pinching from my mind something pretty.

I close my eyes and turn it all inside out a hundred times or more.
Then, and I almost mistake it for wind, the land starts singing back.

Suitcase

We keep our suitcases in the basement.
So I went down to find them, and right before
I'd been praying about abundance,
thankfulness. And I went down and found
the suitcases stacked in the corner—we haven't gone
anywhere lately that required suitcases.
My daughter without a coat and the cold coming,
and when I opened the top suitcase it was full
of winter coats. I'm not even joking. Hand-me-downs
I'd packed away in the summer and forgotten about.
I felt like someone was really seeing me.
I felt playful, almost. I found my old violin, the one I'd given
up lessons for, and I squeaked out a few terrible notes
there in the dark corner of the basement,
the floor made of dirt and the morning still black.
I went upstairs to show my husband
the suitcase full of jackets, and there he was
standing at the window looking up the street
and down, one way and another. What are you looking for?
I asked sweetly, right in the hallway, warm and with a suitcase.
He said he was wondering who was honking, musically,
he said, but wildly, like cars out of control, or geese.

Lamplight, 4 p.m.

There's this section at my favorite store in the mall,
the vacation section, even in winter, even in February,
bathing suits and straw hats, purses you'd only ever wear
on a cruise, too small for money, even.
I read this on one of those decorative wall hangings:
Light serves its purpose when it's in darkness.
I repeat it to my friend (we meet at the mall).
She's trying so hard to help this boy
(she works in the child psychiatric ward). The boy, she says,
sexually abused his young cousin, then killed her, stuffed her
under his mattress, slept on her for weeks before the smell of her
alerted his parents. After she tells me this,
the mall seems more blank, even.
All the stores seem to be trying so hard.

In a picture from 1985, my uncle, since dead, is standing
facing the sun, his eyes squinting, and three faces down
my other uncle, also dead long ago. And it seems so obvious
that everyone in the picture will someday be gone,
but it doesn't make it any less difficult or strange.
There I am in the grass, sitting with my cousins.
My legs folded, I'm smiling toward the sun.
I'm the same age my daughter is now
and with a kitty on my shirt, though I've never
liked cats, but my daughter does. So maybe that's time folding over
on itself again. Out of the seven couples there, only two
are still married: my grandparents and my aunt and uncle.
I'm holding on tightly to the grass, my hands so small,
as if I knew, even then, I could slip off,
fast, like water.

For Valentine's Day my mother-in-law
decorated her big house. She hung a bright red light
inside the front door. One night, a trucker came knocking.
His lights shining beneath his belt buckle.

I keep the door to my office cracked open to let the heat in.
My husband reaches in, hands me a perfect egg on a toast heel.
His arm and the plate of egg are all I can see of him.
Later, he hands me a cup of tea. Then a chocolate, half-eaten.
Each time, only an arm and a dish.
He knows me. These are the most romantic gestures.
I promise, I don't want roses.
I just want to know how to paint them.
And how to find peace under all the pointy thorns of pretty.
If you say pointy thorns out loud,
it makes the lips move in all sorts of directions.
So I wonder what the wind thinks.
I wonder if it likes to move all together,
like a marriage, like a flock: a murmuration.
We are a family now, and there's grace to that.
I like to think that's what the wind thinks.
My husband told me how the wind wanted
to blow the coat off a man but couldn't.
The man only pulled his coat tighter.
The sun tried, too.
Using light and warmth, the sun won.
The coat fell to the sand.
I think, Of course, though I hadn't guessed it at first.

Rural Letter Carrier (Route 18)

The saddest thing is watching
my daughter stand on the edge
of the porch and call for
the neighborhood cat. I'm watching her
from behind, her pajama bottoms
loose in the rump, and the cat
doesn't come. Or the dog wishing
for a walk when there won't be one
because the husband is working
and I am working, and I have more
work on top of that,
and my daughter's stockinged feet
are jammed into her flip-flops,
and I know she's crying now.
Or maybe the saddest thing
is when I come to a door with
a letter to sign for, and the lady
opens it, and a face already sad turns sadder.
Once I had to step over a breathing hose
to get to a lady on a couch,
and I couldn't see where the hose ended.
It stretched on forever, and maybe
it looked a lot like the road
in front of me, and I know exactly
what is up ahead and I am scared.
One day, I knocked on a door,
a package in my arms like a friend
I had been traveling with, and the man
on the other side said, Who is it?
I didn't know what to say, and maybe
that is the saddest thing. I am
the lady who likes your horses.
I am the lady who drove all day
to get here. I am the lady you'll
call in to complain about without once
looking into my eyes and noticing that

I, too, am waiting for the stray,
that I am watching my daughter
turn around after hollering, Fluffy,
again and again, the privet hedges
holding hands and throwing her little shouts
around the yard like all of this is just
a game to play, and I am at the desk
with two computers on in a row.
Behind the door with my package
I said, I am a mother who doesn't know
what to do about her daughter
who is somewhere crying.
I almost always miscommunicate.
So you can imagine what I am doing
with the trees, just me and them,
on a road framed by windows,
their branches hanging with their
little quiet bells of old sadnesses,
and my daughter's tears are like
raindrops on the window between us,
pretty and sad and not a single
thing I can do about any of them.

My Mother Is a Bat

> When they turn the sun on again I'll plant children under it...
> I'll take my mother and soap her up.
> —*Anne Sexton, During the Spring 2020 Pandemic*

Next time I'll do it better.
I promise.

Big Quiet Things

Forever we remember her
on our way to the coast,
in the back seat, quiet
for a million miles,
watching movies with
headphones on and
then, as if a word were
a thing, as if quiet
were an ocean,
and out of it: CRAB!
And years now later,
my husband can say it
or I can say it,
and we are warmed together
even when all around us,
sinking us, pulling us under,
a riptide. And it feels
impossible. And there's
nothing to hold onto.
Silence for a million miles.
Then out of it
a word, and then more where
that one came from,
all washing up, and the sun
warm, the sand
here with us,
waiting with us.

Chakra

> I lie in the dark wondering if this quiet in me now
> is a beginning or an end.
> —*Jack Gilbert*

This morning has been so many days already.
On the phone, I ask about my grandparents.
Right inside that asking fits
a hundred bouts of bad health, each followed by a short reprieve.
The pictures of my childhood are shadows I lie in.
I hang up, and it rings again and again.
I pause down the hallway. Fear,
I fill with it, simple and old,
like a stove pipe with his smoke cloud.
Listen, all the smoke cloud wants is her breath at the top.
Oh, but a freshly lit fire.
Oh, and a hello sweet,
creamy almost. There there, that was easy.
But quick as that an artery clogs and I choke.
I'm going to eat a salad! I scream at the day.
A prayer can happen quickly as that, too.
Energies in color flow up through me and out.
When I walk the sidewalk under
the black lines pulled pole to pole,
my jaw chatters like a funny jar of false teeth.
My daughter bought a snail yesterday because her fish,
he's lonely, and dangerous but too pretty for us to believe that.
She prays to find him alive each morning.
Each morning he's there again like the sea.
Every day, I read to the fish these lines by a man named Vuong:
Once, I came near enough to a man to smell a woman's scent.
I deeply wonder why my mother
couldn't have thought of something better than Jan.
I know the little boats are dangerously out there,
but I ask anyway. And I know the day won't answer
when I ask why she rushed in with her gray covers
when just a minute ago there was nothing there
but my energy between the stars and me.
No clouds at all, I swear.

Bullion

From Fort Knox, KY

The soldiers stood in a firing line
in the brown grasses of February.
Maybe they were just practicing,
maybe they weren't all aiming at me,
quietly walking past to my car,
tiptoeing in my big boots, mid-day,
the sun high, the day warm, as if
someone had shot the gold of
a pretty spring day right into the middle
of winter. Maybe they were all pointing
at me, sneaking past. Unseen I'd hoped.
Some mornings, I tiptoe bootless toward
my husband, lean in for a kiss.
You don't have to tiptoe, he says, but I like to.
I like the quietness of coming in
without him knowing. Or going
out as a shot fired. I turned,
but it was nothing—a blank,
straight into a blank sky.
Some days it feels like no one can see me.
That seems like a good thing.

Unforced Rhythms of Grace

The day my daughter and I stood
under the cell tower, she was still
young enough to believe I could
kiss away her pain, and maybe I can.
Sometimes I believe it too,
that I can pull all my blessings down
like my yoga teacher at the end of class.
Her long and lovely arms reaching
the clouds, she pulls it all down
because who or what wouldn't want to
be invited there? She's beautiful.
My daughter is beautiful, and when she stood
under the cell tower, the clouds floating above,
she said it looked like it was swaying,
like it all was going to come falling down,
and I knew in that instant,
it was up to me to change her mind,
to give her belief and hope about all
that towers over us. But that day I was still
afraid, I wasn't yet sure, and I agreed with her,
my voice simply a noise she heard.
I hope she won't remember.

Goldenrod

On one of my morning walks, I came upon
a man throwing away his roast beef in the bushes.
It was the morning after I woke in the night
to the strange sound of my daughter's
rollerblade rolling backwards off the shelf.
My husband is off to the farmers market.
I keep thinking about the field we passed
on our drive, filled to the edges
with goldenrod, how the flowers went on forever.
Years ago, the night road reached up
and pulled my best friend down into a ditch.
Then she was gone, just like that.
When I woke to the sound of
the rollerblade crashing on the concrete
I thought, Easter Bunny?
Because it was Easter (my thoughts aren't that cute).
When I walk, I think the fancy houses all
have their eyes shut. I'm tempted to cross
onto their lawns, just to see. I'm actually
grateful for so much. We explain to our daughter
where to hide if someone breaks in.
A little hole of dirt space under the kitchen.
It feels like a grave. My mother gets ready
to go to the grocery store. She says,
I'll wear a handkerchief over my mouth and carry a gun.
Here the news is off and the sun is on.
I hung my daughter's fancy white dress
from the basement ceiling. My husband says
it looks like a horror film down there.
Now he is on the roof fighting with the starlings.
I read once that hiding from the world is different
from being at home. On one of my morning
walks, a black cat crossed in front of me
so I walked the other way.
I like when the warmth breaks
through the quiet of a long morning frost.

This Thing Like That

When she was little,
my daughter would pull
a cotton ball from the bag
and place it in the little yard
of her hand, then shelter it
with the roof of her other hand.
She'd whisper into the windows,
I love you, I'll keep you safe.
If there ever were
a happy cotton ball.
Like coming home.
Like pulling off new shoes
at the end of the day.
Like sitting in my flowered chair
beneath the window looking out
and hearing it, suddenly,
almost too quick to catch,
like a car passing,
like wind.

Lamplight, 7:30 p.m.

The food at the hotel took forever,
but we didn't mind.
We had two-and-a-half hours to kill.
But there was a lady there, she was blond.
She was alone with her young blond son.
She kept turning and looking at the kitchen,
as if willing her sandwiches to arrive, and there I was,
caught at the halfway point of her turn.
We kept catching each other in a glance.
Like a light searching through darkness
and finding, for a moment, the wrong thing.
I kept closing my eyes and praying
for the blond lady to get her sandwiches.
I recognized her kind of tired.
The tourists kept checking in.
I heard their suitcases bumping across the tiles.
The lamplight buzzed above us.
The light was so bright it was impossible to see
where it came from, but it didn't matter at all
to either one of us.

Acknowledgements

"Yellow" and "Dear Tuth Fary," Free State Review

"This Thing Like That," "Cupboard," and "We Hold Up the Weight
   That Will Bring Us Down" ("How to Give Credit"), Adanna
   Literary Journal

"Before Bed My Husband Called Me an Old Testament God" and
   "Unforced Rhythms of Grace," Jellybucket

"Wallpaper," Rise Up Review

"For the Curtains and the Wind in the Curtains," Burnside Review

"In All Their Performances," The Shallow Ends

"Rural Letter Carrier," Mom Egg Review

"Anesthesia" and "Somewhere," Inscape

"After Running to My Daughter Late in the Night, She Tells Me Her
   Nightmare is About Snakes, Not Poisonous, and a Little Bit of
   Bears," Heron Tree

"Dragon," Stirring

About the Author

Jan LaPerle's other books include: a volume of poetry, *It Would Be Quiet* (Prime Mincer Press, 2013); an e-chap of flash fiction, *Hush* (Sundress Publications, 2012); a story in verse, *A Pretty Place To Mourn* (BlazeVOX, 2014). She completed her MFA from Southern Illinois University. In 2014 she won an individual artist grant from the Tennessee Arts Commission. She now lives in Kentucky with her husband and daughter, and is a master sergeant in the U.S. Army at Fort Knox.